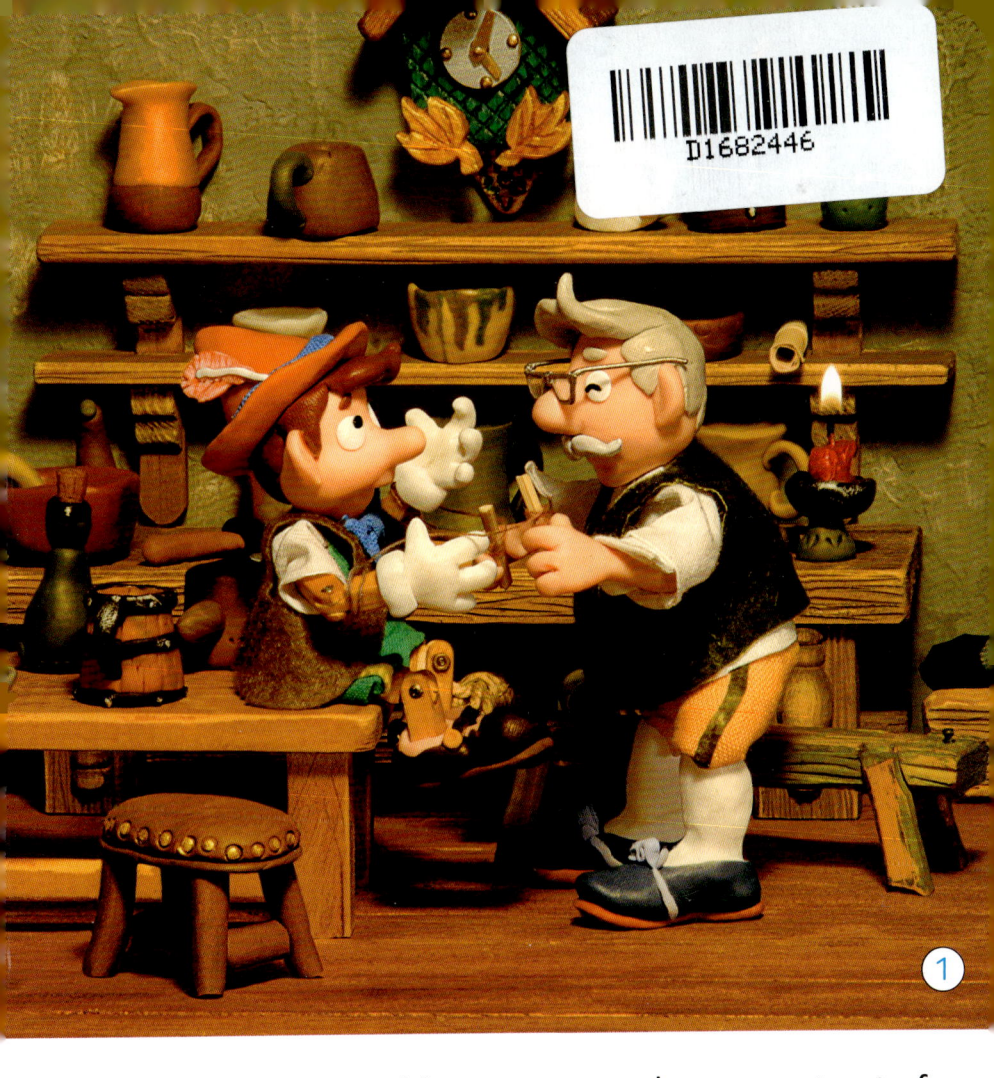

Once upon a time, an old carpenter made a puppet out of a piece of wood. He then attached some strings to the puppet so that he could make him move.

The old carpenter named the puppet Pinocchio. He thought to himself, "How I wish he could become a real boy one day!"

One night, a fairy visited Pinocchio. She waved her magic wand and said, "I'm here to grant the carpenter's wish and bring you to life!"

Then the fairy said to Pinocchio, "If you are honest and brave you will become a real boy, but if you lie your nose will grow long."

Pinocchio didn't listen to the fairy's warning. He was so excited that he started to dance and sing loudly. The old carpenter was woken up by the noise.

When he saw Pinocchio full of life in front of him, the old carpenter was very happy. He treated him as his own son and decided to send him to school.

Before Pinocchio left for school, the old carpenter said, "Be careful on the way there and don't get involved with suspicious characters!"

On his way to school Pinocchio took notice of everything around him. It was all new and interesting. Suddenly, a circus poster caught his attention.

He was very excited. He ran in to the circus to take a look, jumped on the stage, and began to sing and dance. He had completely forgotten about school.

When Pinocchio was bored with the circus, he left and went back out on to the street. There he met the fairy who had brought him to life.

The fairy asked Pinocchio why he hadn't gone to school. He replied that his father had suggested he go and have some fun at the circus.

Pinocchio had told a lie. As the fairy had warned him, his nose grew longer straight away.

Pinocchio continued to wander the streets, and soon he was spotted by two very suspicious characters — a limping fox and a one-eyed cat.

They approached Pinocchio and said to him, "You will be bored at school. Why not come with us and have some fun at the funfair?"

Pinocchio thought this was a great idea, so he followed them to the funfair. Wow! There were lots of things to play with! Pinocchio was very excited.

The limping fox and the one-eyed cat introduced a boy to Pinocchio. The two became friends straight away and started to play games together.

While Pinocchio and his new friend were having a good time, the fox and cat secretly sold them to the boss of the funfair for a bag of gold coins.

Pinocchio and his new friend were treated badly at the funfair, but still they kept on lying. Their noses grew longer and donkey ears grew on their heads.

Eventually, Pinocchio's new friend changed into a donkey and he was sold to a farmer by the owner of the funfair.

Pinocchio was very scared and regretted not listening to his father. He missed him very much.

Just then, the fairy appeared. Pinocchio said to her, "I really want to go back to my father, go to school and be a good boy. Please can you help me?"

Meanwhile, the old carpenter was thinking of his son. He couldn't find him anywhere and was sick with worry.

The good fairy sent Pinocchio home. He apologised for his foolishness and asked his father to forgive him. At once, his long nose and donkey ears disappeared.

Now Pinocchio became a real boy and he lived happily with his father from then on.